For Tiitus and the musical future of all little ones.

Sound Tuition's
Music Notes

The Music Notes Sing ABC is the second book in Sound Tuition's Music Notes series. Book one, Meet the Music Notes introduced the international names for the four most basic music-note durations; whole notes, lasting for four beats; half notes, lasting for two beats; quarter notes, lasting for one beat; and eighth notes, lasting for half of a beat.

The majority of music is made from three elements:
melody (one note played after another);
harmony (notes played together);
rhythm (the duration of notes).

The Music Notes Sing ABC focuses on melody and introduces the first three notes of the international music-notation system; A, B, and C.

The book builds on the ideas contained within Meet the Music Notes, by combining rhythm (the interaction between the lengths of notes) with pitch (the musical height of notes).

As always, throughout the book readers are encouraged to be active learners, and in this way the Sound Tuition Music Notes series is not just a collection of fun stories for children, but it provides a professional and practical education in music.

The Learning Objectives
of
The Music Notes Sing ABC

Keep thinking about the following elements whilst reading the book.

1) The common note names and their values:
whole note—four beats;
half note—two beats;
quarter note—one beat;
eighth note—half of a beat.
• Some countries use different names for the note values—please see page five of Meet the Music Notes.

2) The idea that notes have a quality called *pitch*, which refers to how high or low a sound can be.

3) The use of the voice to sing the first three notes of the international music system; A, B, and C★.

4) The ability to clap the beats "one, and, two, and, three, and, four, and" whilst singing the notes A, B, and C on top of these beats.

★ Please be aware, other systems exist such as *fixed do*, in which the same three notes would be called la, si, and do; la (A), si (B), and do (C). 'Do' is pronounced 'dough' in this system. Anyone interested in expanding their understanding of these systems is advised to investigate solfège, fixed do, and moveable do, as points of departure.

About Pitch

Musical notes are sounds which have a specific musical height. A note's musical height is called its pitch. There are several ways to describe a note's pitch. In other words, there are several different systems for labelling/naming musical notes.

Scientific Pitch Notation

Sound Tuition uses the system known as Scientific Pitch Notation (SPN) throughout its Music Notes series; due to its numerous benefits over other systems. SPN labels all musical notes using the first seven letters of the alphabet (A, B, C, D, E, F, and G) plus a number. These seven letters repeat in a series and a bigger number indicates a higher note. Due to historical reasons, confusingly, the system starts at C_0. Therefore the first four cycles of the series are:
C_0, D_0, E_0, F_0, G_0, A_0, B_0, C_1, D_1, E_1, F_1, G_1, A_1, B_1, C_2, D_2, E_2, F_2, G_2, A_2, B_2, C_3, D_3, E_3, F_3, G_3, A_3, etc.

Which Notes are Higher and Which Notes are Lower?

- Page six reinforces and clarifies the following ideas.
- Bigger numbers are higher; C_2 is higher than C_1.
- Further to the right is higher; F_3 is higher than E_3.
- Remember, the series starts from the note C and not from A. Therefore, A_1 is higher than C_1, and B_2 is higher than G_2.

The Piano as an Example

A piano is a great instrument for easily understanding the labelling system on, because the notes are laid out in a logical order. Also a virtual keyboard/piano is easily downloadable to a mobile device.

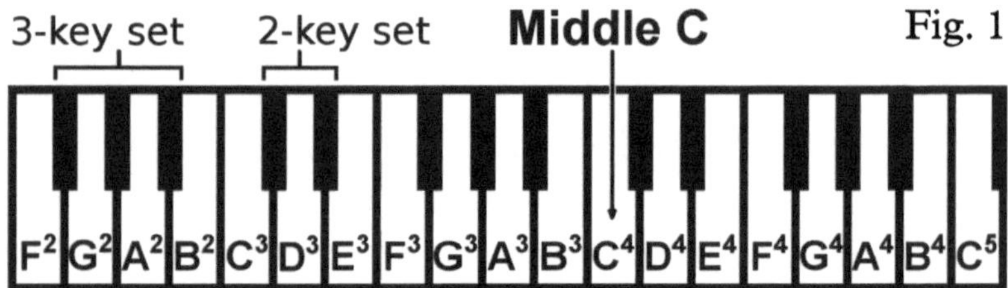

Pianos come in different shapes and sizes, and with a differing number of keys. We are most interested in the number of keys on the piano. Pianos can theoretically have any number of keys, however, the majority have as few as 32 keys, or as many as 88 keys; 88 keys being known as full size. Figure one shows a keyboard diagram for a 32-key piano. It is highly recommended that all readers download a virtual piano to their mobile device. For example, download Sound Tuition's 32-key Virtual Piano; which matches figure one above.

• Play the notes on the virtual keyboard and hear how they get higher the further the note is to the right and lower the further the note is to the left.
• Notice the numbers and that, for example, A_2 is lower in pitch than A_3.
• Notice the diagram starts at F_2. The most important element is to understand the series of notes and then to be able to work out any note, once you know the starting note of the specific keyboard you are using.
• C_4 is called middle C and is used as a reference point.

The Notes We Need

The Music Notes Sing ABC focuses, hopefully not surprisingly, on singing the notes A, B, and C. As can be seen from figure one on page six, there are many As, many Bs, and many Cs.

As a reader, you are encouraged to sing along with all of the examples and exercises within this book. However, everybody has a specific range of musical notes which they can comfortably sing. It is vital that no one damages their voice whilst singing the exercises and examples within this book. For this reason all of the examples, which require the reader to sing a specific note, have been recorded and included in the accompanying app at three different musical heights; A_2–C_3, A_3–C_4, and A_4–C_5. Use the Sound Tuition's 32-key Virtual Piano to play these notes (A_2, B_2, C_3 and then A_3, B_3, C_4 and finally A_4, B_4, C_5). Sing along with these notes using the sound 'la' and find the ABC set which is most comfortable for you. Then use this specific ABC set whilst singing the exercises within this book. There is no need to sing if you do not wish to.

What if I Cannot Sing?

Singing comes very naturally for some and is unspeakably difficult for others. Do not worry if you feel you cannot find any of the As, Bs, or Cs with your voice. Anything can be learnt with help, patience, and practice. Start by just listening to the audio examples in the app and enjoy reading the book. A professional singing teacher is the answer if you need more help.

Audio Symbol

Throughout the book the symbol 🔊 can be seen next to a page and exercise number. This corresponds to the accompanying audio within the app. For example:

$$\text{P. 16 Ex. 1 } A_2\text{–}C_3$$
$$\text{P. 16 Ex. 2 } A_3\text{–}C_4$$
$$\text{P. 16 Ex. 3 } A_4\text{–}C_5$$

This would mean that the audio is found on the page 16 section of the app and contains three different audio examples. The pitch (height) of the notes is indicated by the small numbers next to the note names; A_2–C_3 being the lowest and A_4–C_5 being the highest.

App-Free Reading

This book is enhanced by the use of the accompanying app. The app provides all of the exercises and examples from the book in audio format. This gives readers the ability to hear how the singing should sound and to sing along with the examples to support practice and learning. However, should anyone for any reason not wish to use the app when reading the book then it is advised that readers practise singing the notes A, B, and C, until they are confident that they can recall these sounds and use them when reading the book. Please watch Sound Tuition's, The Music Notes Sing ABC App-Free-Reading video, to see how the book can be read without the use of the app. However, the app is fantastic and thoroughly recommended to anyone wanting the best musical education.

Middle C and the Octave

Middle C was mentioned briefly at the bottom of page six. C_4 is called middle C because it is the C nearest to the middle of an 88-key (full-sized) piano and it is the fourth C on an 88-key piano. Notice the ABC sets used throughout this book are the set nearest middle C and then the ABC set one series below and one series above this set; each series of A, B, C, D, E, F, and G is called an *octave* in music. A full-sized piano has a little over seven octaves of notes.

Do Not Strain Your Voice

It is vital that anyone singing along with the exercises and examples within this book does not damage their voice. It is recommended that the sound 'la' be used when starting to sing and focusing on creating natural, relaxed sounds. If at any point you feel discomfort then stop singing and seek the advice of a professionally qualified singing teacher. Singing must be a joyful, stress and strain free, activity.

Additional Tools

Download Sound Tuition's The Music Notes Sing ABC app as well as Sound Tuition's 32-key Virtual Piano app to your mobile device and visit Sound Tuition's website for the best musical education possible.

www.SoundTuition.com

In the land of Stave, not so far away live the Music Notes.

Whole Note, Half Note, Quarter Note, and Eighth Note.

Whole Note's favourite number is four.

Half Note's favourite number is two.

Quarter Note's favourite number is one.

Eighth Note's favourite number is a half.

Can you write their names under their pictures?

2
4
1/2
1

The Music Notes would like to sing with you.

When we sing, the sounds we make can be at different heights.

Listen to Quarter Note making a low sound and then a high sound.

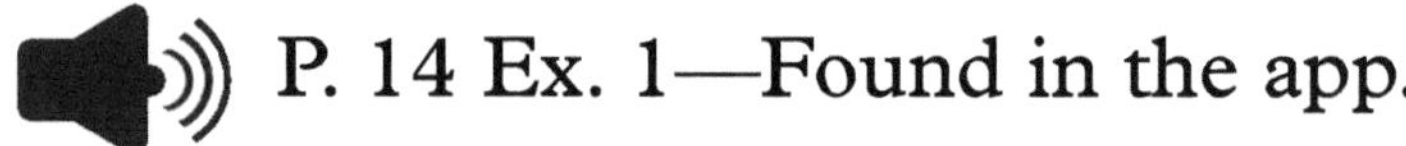 P. 14 Ex. 1—Found in the app.

Can you make a low sound and then a high sound?

La!
La!

Pitch is the word we use to describe how high or low a sound is.

Listen to Quarter Note make three sounds at different pitches (heights).

🔊 P. 16 Ex. 1

Can you make three sounds at different pitches (heights)?

La!
La!
La!

Quarter Note wants to make the three sounds again, but this time give the sounds names.

Listen to Quarter Note sing the three sounds and call them A, B, and C.

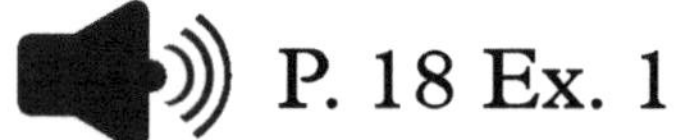 P. 18 Ex. 1

A
B
C

Can you sing A, B, and C along with Quarter Note?

Try to make the same sounds; using 'la'.

If these sounds are too low or too high for you then try singing the same sounds either higher or lower.

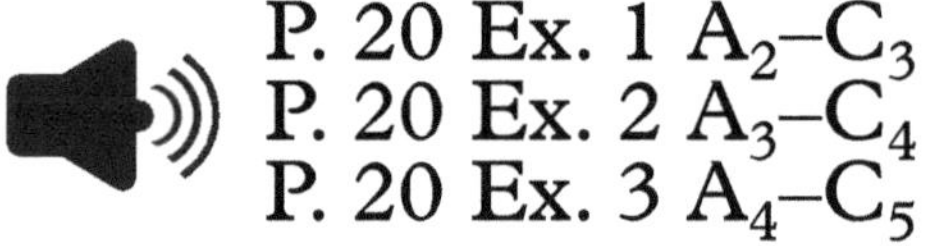

P. 20 Ex. 1 A_2–C_3
P. 20 Ex. 2 A_3–C_4
P. 20 Ex. 3 A_4–C_5

Find a height at which you can sing comfortably. Do not strain your voice.

If you feel discomfort then stop singing and just listen to the Music Notes singing.

A
B
C
Sing
with me!

Whole Note wants to know
if you remember the Music
Notes' favourite numbers?

Whole Note's favourite number is _____.

Half Note's favourite number is _____.

Quarter Note's favourite number is _____.

Eighth Note's favourite number is _____.

Half Note wants to know if you
remember the word to describe
how high or low a sound is?

The word to describe the height
of a sound is called ___________.

The Music Notes would like to play a singing and clapping game with you.

Half Note starts by singing A, B, and C, whilst clapping Half Note's favourite number; two.

Can you sing and clap at the same time like Half Note?

Remember to use the pitches A, B, and C, that are comfortable for you to sing.

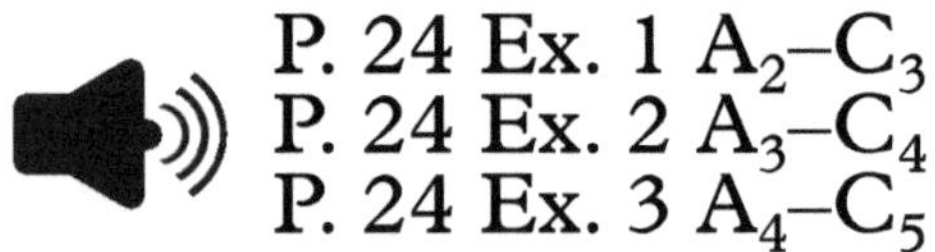

P. 24 Ex. 1 A_2–C_3
P. 24 Ex. 2 A_3–C_4
P. 24 Ex. 3 A_4–C_5

1 2 1 2 1 2
A
B
C

Next it is Quarter Note's turn.

Quarter Note sings A, B, and C, whilst clapping their favourite number; one.

P. 26 Ex. 1 A_2–C_3
P. 26 Ex. 2 A_3–C_4
P. 26 Ex. 3 A_4–C_5

Notice Quarter Note claps only once whilst singing each sound.

Can you sing A, B, and C, whilst clapping once along with each sound?

Remember never to strain your voice!

1 1 1
A B C
- 27 -

Eighth Note wants to use their favourite number whilst clapping; a half.

Each clap can be called a **beat**.

Do you remember how to count half beats from the Meet the Music Notes book?

We use the word "and". Count out loud with Eighth Note and clap on every number and every "and".

"One, and, two, and, three, and, four, and.
One, and, two, and, three, and, four, and.
One, and, two, and, three, and, four, and.
One, and, two, and, three, and, four, and."

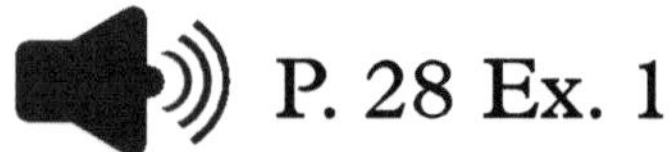 P. 28 Ex. 1

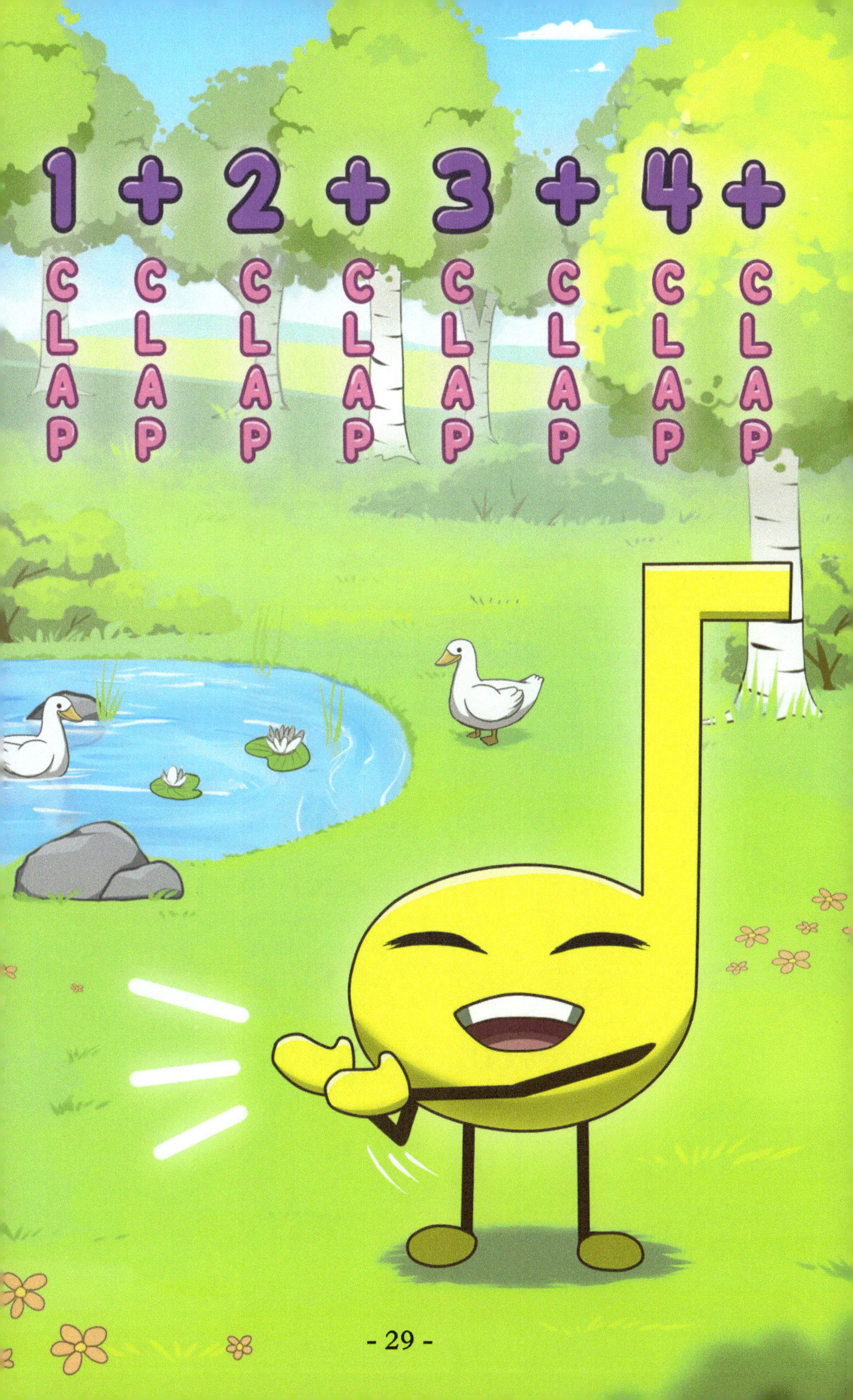
1 + 2 + 3 + 4 +
CLAP CLAP CLAP CLAP CLAP CLAP CLAP CLAP

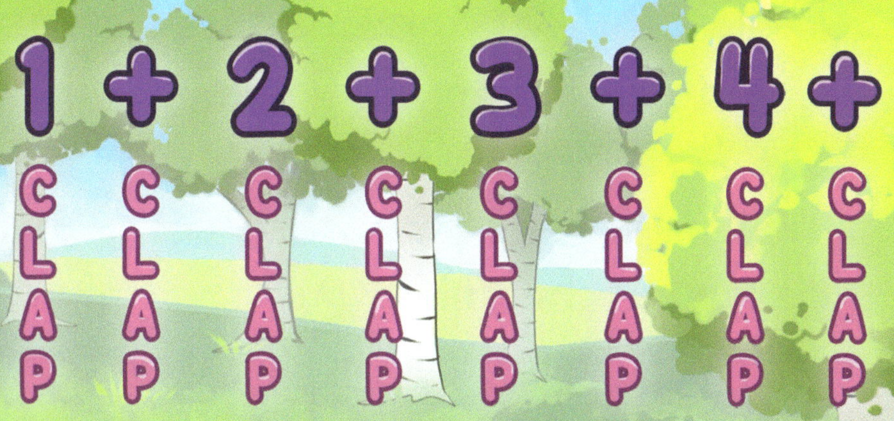

Half Note wants to play the singing and clapping game again.

This time Half Note wants to clap all of the half beats.

Clap:	1	+	2	+	3	+	4	+
Sing:	A				B			

Clap:	1	+	2	+	3	+	4	+
Sing:	C				Rest			

P. 30 Ex. 1 A_2–C_3
P. 30 Ex. 2 A_3–C_4
P. 30 Ex. 3 A_4–C_5

How many half beats does Half Note clap for each sound?

Half Note claps ___ half beats for each sound.

The '+'s are the 'and's from page 28.

1 + 2 + 3 + 4 +   1 + 2 + 3 + 4 +
A
B
C

Quarter Note wants to play the singing and clapping game again.

This time Quarter Note wants to clap all of the half beats.

Clap:	1	+	2	+	3	+	4	+
Sing:	A		B		C		Rest	

P. 32 Ex. 1 A_2–C_3
P. 32 Ex. 2 A_3–C_4
P. 32 Ex. 3 A_4–C_5

How many half beats does Quarter Note clap for each sound?

Quarter Note claps ___ half beats for each sound.

1 + 2 + 3 + 4 +
A
B
C

Eighth Note, who has been waiting so patiently, would now like to play the singing and clapping game.

Eighth Note's favourite number is a half and so they clap and sing on all of the half beats.

Clap:	1	+	2	+	3	+	4	+
Sing:	A	B	C	Rest				

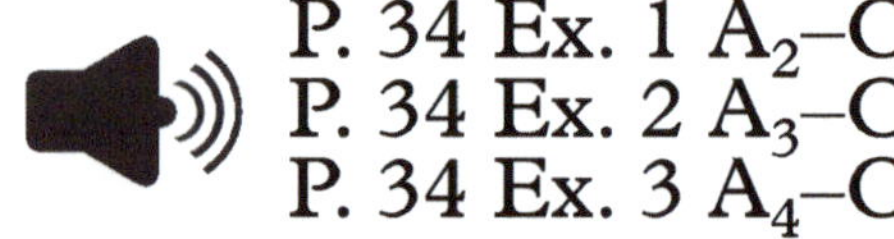

P. 34 Ex. 1 A_2–C_3
P. 34 Ex. 2 A_3–C_4
P. 34 Ex. 3 A_4–C_5

1 + 2 + 3 + 4 +
A
B
C

Eighth Note sings A, B, and C so quickly that they would like to play the game again.

This time Eighth Note sings A, B, C, B, A, B, C.

Clap:	1	+	2	+	3	+	4	+
Sing:	A	B	C	B	A	B	C	Rest

P. 36 Ex. 1 A_2–C_3
P. 36 Ex. 2 A_3–C_4
P. 36 Ex. 3 A_4–C_5

Can you feel the pitch of the notes change as Eighth Note sings up to the highest note and then down to the lowest?

Which note is the highest? ___.
Which note is the lowest? ___.

1 + 2 + 3 + 4 +
A B C B A B C

Half Note and Quarter Note want to play the singing and clapping game together.

Half Note sings the first A, then Quarter Note sings the B and the C.

They both clap together; all of the half beats.

Clap:	1	+	2	+	3	+	4	+
HN:	A				Rest			
QN:	Rest				B		C	

P. 38 Ex. 1 A_2–C_3
P. 38 Ex. 2 A_3–C_4
P. 38 Ex. 3 A_4–C_5

1 + 2 + 3 + 4 +
4
4
A
B
C

Half Note and Quarter Note
want to play the singing and
clapping game together again.

This time Quarter Note sings the
A and the B, and then Half Note
sings the C.

They both clap together; all of
the half beats.

Clap:	1	+	2	+	3	+	4	+
HN:	Rest				C			
QN:	A		B		Rest			

P. 40 Ex. 1 A_2–C_3
P. 40 Ex. 2 A_3–C_4
P. 40 Ex. 3 A_4–C_5

1 + 2 + 3 + 4 +
4
4
A
B
C

Eighth Note would like to play the game with Quarter Note.

Eighth Note starts by singing up and down the sounds—A, B, C, B—and then Quarter Note sings A and then B.

Clap:	1	+	2	+	3	+	4	+
EN:	A	B	C	B	Rest			
QN:	Rest				A		B	

P. 42 Ex. 1 A_2–C_3
P. 42 Ex. 2 A_3–C_4
P. 42 Ex. 3 A_4–C_5

Do you remember what their favourite numbers are and why Eighth Note sings on every half beat but Quarter Note sings only every two half beats?

1 + 2 + 3 + 4 +
4
4
A B C B A B

Finally, Half Note, Quarter Note, and Eighth Note would all like to play the singing and clapping game together.

Half Note starts and sings one A. Next Quarter Note sings one B. Eighth Note sings one C and one B. Then Whole Note surprises everyone and sings one long A, lasting for four beats, at the end of the game.

Clap:	1	+	2	+	3	+	4	+
HN:	A				Rest			
QN:	Rest				B		Rest	
EN:	Rest						C	B

Clap:	1	+	2	+	3	+	4	+
WN:	A							

P. 44 Ex. 1 A_2–C_3
P. 44 Ex. 2 A_3–C_4
P. 44 Ex. 3 A_4–C_5

1 + 2 + 3 + 4 + 1 + 2 + 3 + 4 +
4
4
A
B
C
B
A

Sound Tuition's Music Notes had a wonderful time singing and clapping with you today.

Can you remember how many half beats fit into each of their favourite numbers?

Whole Note's favourite number is __ and __ half beats can fit into it.

Half Note's favourite number is __ and __ half beats can fit into it.

Quarter Note's favourite number is __ and __ half beats can fit into it.

Eighth Note's favourite number is __ and __ half beat can fit into it.

The Music Notes wish you a good day and look forward to playing games with you again.

Become a Great Musician
Writing A, B, C

Can you copy the notes A, B, and C in the exercises on this page; so that they look identical to the examples?

Exercise One: Writing the Note A_4

P. 48 Ex. 1a A_2
P. 48 Ex. 1b A_3
P. 48 Ex. 1c A_4

Exercise Two: Writing the Note B_4

P. 48 Ex. 2a B_2
P. 48 Ex. 2b B_3
P. 48 Ex. 2c B_4

Exercise Three: Writing the Note C_5

P. 48 Ex. 3a C_3
P. 48 Ex. 3b C_4
P. 48 Ex. 3c C_5

Sing the music you have written; sing four As, four Bs, and four Cs. Make sure you are relaxed when singing.

Become a Great Musician
Playing With A, B, C

Can you copy the patterns in the exercises on this page; so that they look identical to the examples?

Exercise One

P. 49 Ex. 1a A$_2$–C$_3$
P. 49 Ex. 1b A$_3$–C$_4$
P. 49 Ex. 1c A$_4$–C$_5$

Exercise Two

P. 49 Ex. 2a A$_2$–C$_3$
P. 49 Ex. 2b A$_3$–C$_4$
P. 49 Ex. 2c A$_4$–C$_5$

Exercise Three

P. 49 Ex. 3a A$_2$–C$_3$
P. 49 Ex. 3b A$_3$–C$_4$
P. 49 Ex. 3c A$_4$–C$_5$

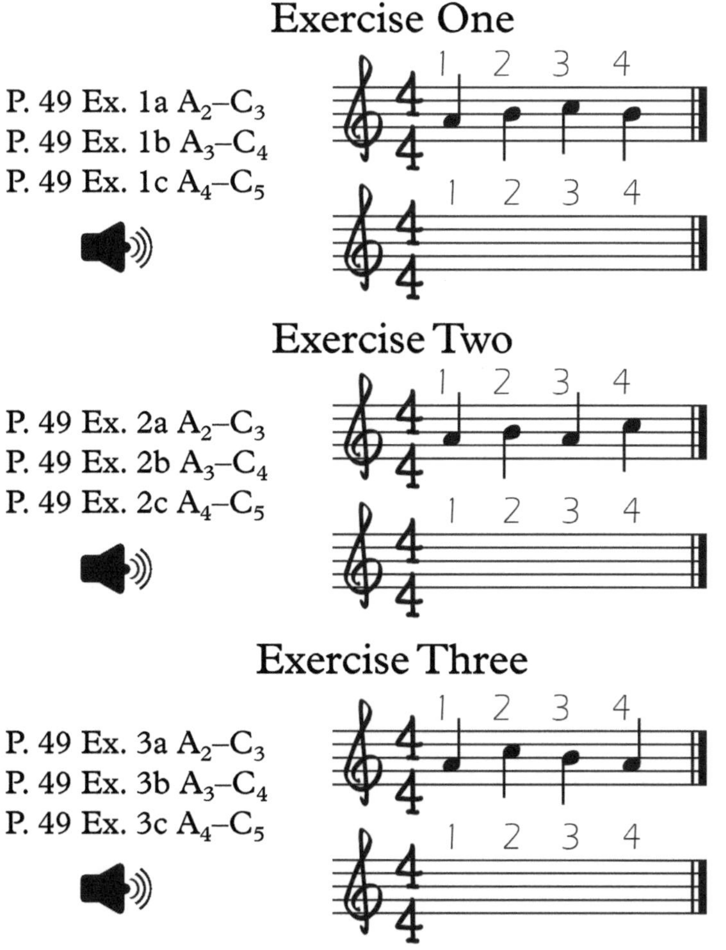

Sing the music you have written. Sing along with the app and use the pitches that are comfortable for you to sing. Do not strain your voice.

Become a Great Musician
Create Your Own Tunes

Can you use the notes A, B, and C to write down and sing your own tunes; like the exercises on page 49?

Can you use whole notes, half notes, quarter notes, and eighth notes? How many different ways can you fill the four beats of a bar?

Join Sound Tuition's
Music Notes on Their Next Adventure in
The Music Notes Write Music

www.ingramcontent.com/pod-product-compliance
Lightning Source LLC
Chambersburg PA
CBHW040926110726
48006CB00001B/86